THE GREATEST
Choral Classics

EIGHTEEN OF THE BEST LOVED CHORUSES FOR MIXED VOICES
SELECTED WITH INTRODUCTORY NOTES BY BRIAN KAY

NOVELLO
LONDON

Orchestral material for the following pieces is available for hire, as separate items, from the Publisher:

BACH	O Jesus when I come to die
BERLIOZ	The Shepherds' Farewell
BRAHMS	How lovely are all Thy dwellings
ELGAR	Give unto the Lord (*Psalm 29*)
FRANCK	Panis angelicus
HANDEL	Zadok the Priest
HAYDN	Insanæ et vanæ curæ
MENDELSSOHN	Hear my prayer
MOZART	Ave verum Corpus
PARRY	Blest pair of Sirens
PARRY	I was glad
SCHUBERT	Sanctus

NOV 072515
ISBN 07119-8831-5

Cover illustration: The Vienna Musikverein by Auguste Mandlick (1860-1934)
Fine Art Photographic Library Ltd by Courtesy of Galerie Berko
Photograph of Brian Kay © BBC

Published in Great Britain by Novello Publishing Limited
Head office: 14-15 Berners Street, London, W1T 3LJ
Tel +44 (0)20 7434 0066 Fax +44 (0)20 7287 6329

Sales and Hire: Music Sales Distribution Centre
Newmarket Road, Bury St Edmunds, Suffolk, IP33 3YB
Tel +44 (0)1284 702600 Fax +44 (0)1284 768301

Web: www.musicsales.com
e-mail: music@musicsales.co.uk

Music setting by Stave Origination

Contents

INTRODUCTION

"Since singing is so good a thing, I wish all men would learne to sing" – so wrote the great sixteenth-century English composer William Byrd, who could have had no idea the extent to which amateur choral singing would become an essenti... ...is currently art of our musical life. Although the Victorian heyday of ch............ of the past, when every ....y proudly supported its own choral and orchestral concerts, there is healthy evidence that more and more of us are turning again to singing in choirs, as a foil to our increasingly hectic and computerised lives at the start of the third millennium.

The Choir of the Year competition which takes place in Great Britain every other year produces more singers each time, with well over 12,000 taking part in the year 2000. The televising of the event has changed the way people appear on the platform, with more and more choirs learning their music by heart and indulging in stage presentation that does much to eradicate the potentially fusty image that choral music has sometimes suffered from in the past. It has also meant an increasing sense of adventure in the choice of music and the building of programmes, and the Novello Choral Programme is a major contributor to this process of ever-widening repertoire.

The important thing in my experience with choirs and audiences is to introduce as much variety as possible within the established concert formulae. The 'highlights' culture has also produced a desire among listeners for as widely-mixed a selection as possible and the reason behind this volume – and its companion volumes – is two-fold. It introduces choirs to extracts from some of the greatest works ever composed for choral voices, in the hope of leading on to the complete works. At the same time, it gives choirs an opportunity to use one volume to present a serendipitous selection of choral gems in a single concert, with the hope that it will also lead audiences to investigate further the very special experience and thrill which complete oratorios uniquely offer. Where orchestral parts are required, these are now available for each individual movement included here, without having to hire the complete works. The availability of such a collection as this should hopefully inspire more people to fulfil the wish so fervently expressed by William Byrd five centuries ago.

Brian Kay

MISERERE MEI, DEUS *Gregorio Allegri* (1582-1652)

Gregorio Allegri was a member of the choir of the Sistine Chapel in Rome and his setting of Psalm 51 was sung there annually during Holy Week on three consecutive days. The authorities were keenly aware of the magnificence of the music, and the manuscript remained a closely guarded secret for many years. Eventually it became more easily accessible, partly the result of a visit to the chapel by the 14-year-old Mozart, who wrote out the score from memory after hearing it just once.

In a choir of many voices, antiphonal effects can be achieved by creating space between the three main choral bodies – the tenors and basses singing the plainchant, the main choir, and a solo quartet. Even without this, Allegri's *Miserere* remains a jewel in the crown of any choral collection.

O JESUS, WHEN I COME TO DIE *Johann Sebastian Bach* (1685-1750)

Bach's great settings of the *St Matthew* and *St John Passions* are for many the most deeply spiritual choral and orchestral works in the repertoire. With a mixture of high drama and intense meditation, Bach's settings of the Passion story unfold in a way that is both human and divine, reflecting the composer's own profound belief as well as his God-given musical genius. This chorale from the *St John Passion* follows the final chorus and ends the work with an uplifting feeling of hope in the resurrection.

AVE MARIA *Bach-Gounod*

Although there may well have been a few raised eyebrows when Charles Gounod (1818-93) added his counter-melody to the Prelude in C from the first book of Bach's collection of keyboard pieces known as 'The 48', there's no doubt that the resultant setting of the *Ave Maria* as a solo song proved enormously popular. This arrangement takes the whole thing a stage further, by fleshing out the harmonies for choral voices in a way that by no means stretches vocal range, and preserves the solemn dignity of the original.

THE SHEPHERDS' FAREWELL *Hector Berlioz* (1803-69)

This much-loved chorus – often sung on its own as a Christmas carol – comes from the beginning of the second part of Berlioz's *The Childhood of Christ*. In it, the Shepherds assemble before the manger and bid farewell to the Holy Family before its flight into Egypt. The music for this chorus started out as an organ piece, and it was only when a friend pointed out its 'pastoral naïve mysticism' to the composer that Berlioz added appropriate words, thereby sowing the seeds of what eventually became the complete oratorio.

HOW LOVELY ARE ALL THY DWELLINGS *Johannes Brahms* (1833-97)

When Brahms composed his *German Requiem* in the late 1860s, he was concerned not so much with peace for the souls of the departed as with comfort for the bereaved. He selected his own texts from the Holy Scriptures, underlining his belief that when the trumpets sound for us on the other side, they are not there to summon us to the Day of Judgement, but rather to underline the hope of reunion and resurrection after death. With that in mind, he chose words for this central movement which express joy in the certainty of our eventually reaching the 'blest courts of the Lord'.

LOCUS ISTE *Anton Bruckner* (1824-96)

Simplicity is the keynote in Bruckner's setting of the Gradual text *Locus iste* – 'This place has been made by God: it is a sacrament beyond praise and reproof'. It is the product of a naturally humble and devoutly religious man. The music represents the other side of the coin from his massive symphonic writings. Here, in a simple expression of faith, he allows himself to indulge in adventurous harmonies in the middle, surrounded by a beginning and ending which are models of restrained serenity.

AVE VERUM *Edward Elgar* (1857-1934)

Elgar's setting of the *Ave verum* was a re-working of the *Pie Jesu* which he had originally written in memory of his boyhood employer, the solicitor William Allen. He later added an *Ave Maria* and an *Ave maris stella* to create a three-part Opus 2. When he sent them to Novellos, he added a note saying "They are tender little plants so treat them kindly whatever is their fate". As with many of the works included in this choral selection, it is the simplicity of the setting that makes it so effective.

GIVE UNTO THE LORD *Edward Elgar*

In contrast with the simplicity of his setting of *Ave verum*, Elgar's *Give unto the Lord*, which sets the words of Psalm 29, is on a much grander scale altogether. It was written (originally for choir, organ and orchestra) at the request of Sir George Martin – the organist at St Paul's Cathedral – for the 200th anniversary of the Sons of the Clergy, which was celebrated there in 1914. The music is on a similar scale to the great choruses in Elgar's oratorios *The Apostles* and *The Kingdom*, and as with all the composer's scores, everything he wants is clearly marked – every subtlety of dynamic, every accent, every effective gesture – offered as a guide to achieving a perfect performance.

CANTIQUE DE JEAN RACINE *Gabriel Fauré* (1845-1924)

Fauré composed this wonderfully peaceful setting of the *Cantique de Jean Racine* as a competition piece while he was still a student at the Ecole Niedermeyer in Paris, and not surprisingly, it won first prize! The gently flowing melodic style shows that even at the age of twenty, his own sense of direction was well established, and that he was already creating the sort of personal response to words which would eventually make his *Requiem* one of the most popular.

PANIS ANGELICUS *César Franck* (1822-90)

The mystery of God made man, who becomes the bread of life in the sacrament is the subject of this communion motet, and the setting by Franck is one of his best-known works. It was originally written as a tenor solo and male chorus, and later incorporated into his *Mass for Three Voices*, but retains its sense of simplicity in Kenneth Downing's arrangement for accompanied four-part choir.

ZADOK THE PRIEST *George Frideric Handel* (1685-1759)

This is the most famous of all coronation anthems – composed for the anointing of George II in 1727, and sung at every coronation service in London since then. It is richly scored for both voices and instruments, and works equally well with a small church choir or a large choral society – and indeed with anything in between. The chorus's massive first entry – after the gradual build-up which precedes it – is one of the most dramatic outbursts in all choral music, and having reached that glorious moment, Handel then retains the sense of excitement right through to the final *Alleluia, Amen*. If a choir is too small to divide all the parts satisfactorily, then it is possible to perform this anthem omitting the second alto and first bass parts.

INSANÆ ET VANÆ CURÆ *Joseph Haydn* (1732-1809)

This surprisingly little-known anthem by Haydn comes originally from his oratorio 'Il ritorno di Tobia' and it seems likely that Haydn approved of its being extracted, and used in this form, with new words added for general use. It gives any choir the opportunity to show its colours, with contrasting sections (each repeated) in which Haydn balances dramatic outburst with a much more lyrical singing. The role of the accompanying organist is also vital to the success and enjoyment of any performance.

HEAR MY PRAYER *Felix Mendelssohn* (1809-47)

Ever since Ernest Lough made a justly famous recording of Mendelssohn's *Hear my prayer* as a chorister in the Temple Church Choir in the late 1920s, this delightful setting has enjoyed enormous popularity for any choir that can happily boast a fine treble or soprano soloist. It contains both beauty and drama, as the words dictate, with anguished singing in the face of the godless enemy, and the most lyrical sense of longing in the final section *O for the wings of a dove*.

AVE VERUM CORPUS *Wolfgang Amadeus Mozart* (1756-91)

This concise choral gem was composed right at the end of Mozart's short life, but unlike the famously unfinished *Requiem*, it is absolutely complete, and says everything it needs to say in the shortest possible span. It's apparent simplicity belies the perfection of its shape and substance, with astonishing subtlety of modulation, a glorious arch-like shape, and vocal lines which lie in the most comfortable part of all four voices.

BLEST PAIR OF SIRENS *C.H.H. Parry* (1848-1918)

Of the many choral works both large and small which were composed by Sir Charles Hubert Hastings Parry, his setting of Milton's *Blest pair of Sirens* remains – alongside *Jerusalem* and the coronation anthem *I was glad* – his best-known and most popular. Its full orchestration and rich writing for eight-part choir make a tremendous impression in performance, and although it is often said that this music resembles Elgar's at its noblest and best, it is important to remember which composer came first.

I WAS GLAD *C.H.H. Parry*

Parry wrote his stirring anthem *I was glad* for the coronation of Edward VII in 1902, and it has been sung at every coronation since. It occurs in the service at the moment when the monarch enters the Abbey, hence the cries of '*Vivat*' with which he or she is traditionally greeted by the Scholars of Westminster School. When the anthem is sung out of context, it is possible to omit this section, as marked in the score, and to continue with the words of the psalm. Parry responds to those words in a variety of ways, with martial music to begin with, a double-choir section to underline the strength of Jerusalem, a *dolce* setting of the prayer for peace, and a rousing climax which sends the highest voices jubilantly to the top of the range.

GOD SO LOVED THE WORLD *John Stainer* (1840-1901)

When Sir John Stainer composed *The Crucifixion* in the late 1880s, he followed Bach's shining example by incorporating into his 'Meditation on the Sacred Passion of the Holy Redeemer' congregational hymns, with the intention – as Bach's had been with his many chorales in the *St Matthew* and *St John Passions* – that all the people should be involved in the story. But he also wrote some fine set pieces for the choir to sing, of which *God so loved the world* is the most profoundly moving – an effect achieved by the divine simplicity of its word-setting.

MISERERE MEI, DEUS

Psalm li, 1-20

GREGORIO ALLEGRI
edited by George Guest

4

6

TENORS and BASSES

[*mf*]

Avérte fáciem túam a peccátis mé — — is:

et ómnes iniquitátes mé — as dé — le.

66 SOPRANO 1
[*mp*]

Cor mun-dum cre - a in me de — — — — — —

SOPRANO 2
[*mp*]

Cor mun-dum cre - a in me___ de — — — — — —

ALTO [*mp*]

Cor mun-dum cre - a in me de — — — — — —

BASS [*mp*]

Cor mun-dum cre - a in me de — — — — — —

70

— — — us: et spi-ri-tum re-ctum in-no-va in vi - sce - ri-bus

— — — us: et spi-ri-tum re-ctum in-no-va in vi - sce - ri-bus me-

— — — us: et spi-ri-tum re-ctum in-no-va in vi - sce - ri-bus

— — — us: et spi-ri-tum re-ctum in-no-va in vi - sce - ri-bus

10

me — — — — — — — — — is.

is.

me — — — — — — — — is.

me — — — — — — — is.

TENORS and
BASSES
[mf]
Ne projícias ma a fácie tu — a.

et spiritum sánctum túum ne áu — fe — ras a me.

SOPRANO 1
[mf]
3   3
Red-de mi – hi lae-ti-ti-am sa-lu-ta — ris tu — — —

SOPRANO 2
[mf]
3   3
Red-de mi – hi lae-ti-ti-am sa-lu-ta — ris tu — —

ALTO [mf]
3   3
Red-de mi – hi lae-ti-ti-am sa-lu-ta — ris tu — — —

TENOR
[mf]
3   3
Red-de mi – hi lae-ti-ti-am sa-lu-ta-ris tu — — —

BASS [mf]
3   3
Red-de mi – hi lae-ti-ti-am sa-lu-ta — ris tu — —

12

TENORS and BASSES

Docébo iníquos vías tú - as: et ímpii ad te con - ver - tén - tur.

SOPRANO 1

Li - be - ra me de san-guin-i-bus, De - us, De-us sa - lu - tis

SOPRANO 2

Li - be - ra me de san-guin-i-bus, De - us, De-us sa - lu - tis ____

ALTO

Li - be - ra me de san-guin-i-bus, De - us, De-us sa - lu - tis

BASS

Li - be - ra me de san-guin-i-bus, De - us, De-us sa - lu - tis

me - - - - - - æ:

me - - - - - - æ:

me - - - - - - æ:

me - - - - - - æ:

et ex-sul-ta-bit lin-gua me-a jus-ti - ti-am tu - -

et ex-sul-ta-bit lin-gua me-a jus-ti - ti-am tu - -

et ex-sul-ta-bit lin-gua me-a jus-ti - ti-am tu - -

et ex-sul-ta-bit lin-gua me-a jus-ti - ti-am tu - -

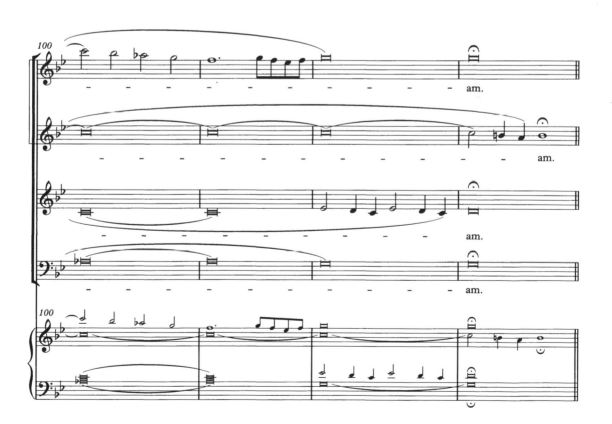

- - - - - - - am.

- - - - - - - am.

- - - - am.

- - - - - - am.

14

18

**Questo ultimo verso si canta Adagio e Piano,
smorzando a poco a poco l'armonia**

O JESUS, WHEN I COME TO DIE

from *St. John Passion (Passio secundum Johannem,* BWV 245)

Text by
Martin Schalling

JOHANN SEBASTIAN BACH
edited in a new English version by Neil Jenkins

AVE MARIA

BACH - GOUNOD
arr. Henry Geehl

THE SHEPHERDS' FAREWELL

from *The Childhood of Christ (L'Enfance du Christ)*

English words by
Paul England

HECTOR BERLIOZ, Op.25

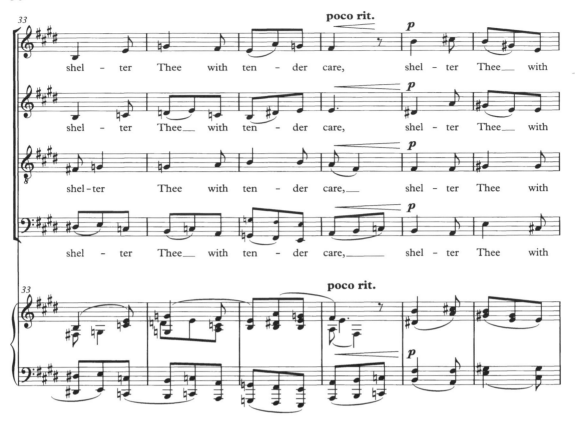

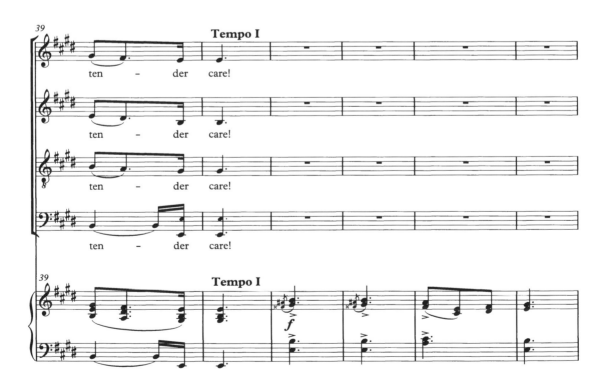

-get not us who lin - ger here! May the

- get not___ us who lin - ger here! May the

-get not us who lin - ger here! May

- get___ not us___ who lin - ger here! May

shep - herd's low - ly call - ing, ev - er to Thy

shep - herd's low - ly call - ing, ev - er to Thy

the shep-herd's low-ly call - ing, ev - er to Thy

the shep-herd's low-ly call - ing, ev - er to Thy

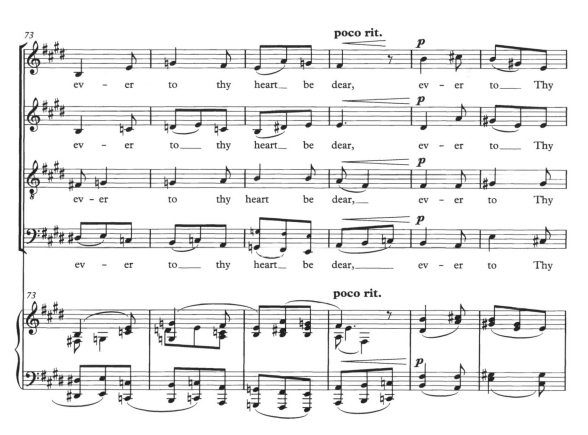

father, mother mild! Guard ye well your Heav'n - ly

Trea-sure, the Prince of Peace, the Ho - ly Child! God go

HOW LOVELY ARE ALL THY DWELLINGS

from *A German Requiem (Ein deutsches Requiem)*

JOHANNES BRAHMS, Op.45

Revised with a new English translation by Michael Pilkington

Psalm lxxxiv, 1,2,4

48

56

dwell - - - - ings fair!
Woh - - - - nun - gen!

dwell - - - - ings fair!
Woh - - - - nun - gen!

dwell - - - - ings fair!
Woh - - - - nun - gen!

dwell - - - - ings fair!
Woh - - - - nun - gen!

dim.

p

Ped.

LOCUS ISTE

ANTON BRUCKNER

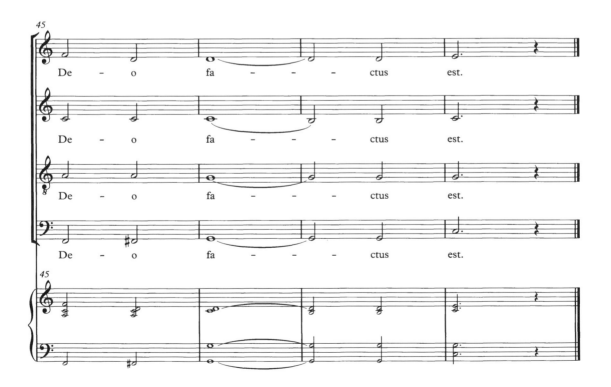

AVE VERUM

EDWARD ELGAR, Op.2 No.1

To my friend Sir George C. Martin

GIVE UNTO THE LORD

Psalm xxix

EDWARD ELGAR, Op.74

74

* Boys (Soprano 2) with Altos

Gt. to Ped. off.

* Boys (Soprano 2) with Altos

* Soprano 2 with Altos

* Boys (Soprano 2) with Altos

CANTIQUE DE JEAN RACINE

Text by
Jean Racine

English words by
Sarah Leftwich

GABRIEL FAURÉ, Op. 11
edited by Desmond Ratcliffe

ORGAN
or
PIANO

92

PANIS ANGELICUS

CÉSAR FRANCK
arr. Kenneth Downing

110

ZADOK THE PRIEST

I Kings i, 39-40

GEORGE FRIDERIC HANDEL
edited by Donald Burrows

No. 1   Chorus ZADOK THE PRIEST

© 2001 Novello & Company Limited

112

[Orchestral bass continues in quaver rhythm]

No. 2   Chorus AND ALL THE PEOPLE REJOIC'D

No. 3   Chorus GOD SAVE THE KING

118

124

INSANÆ ET VANÆ CURÆ

JOSEPH HAYDN

138

144

HEAR MY PRAYER

English words
adapted from
Psalm lv by
William Bartholomew

FELIX MENDELSSOHN

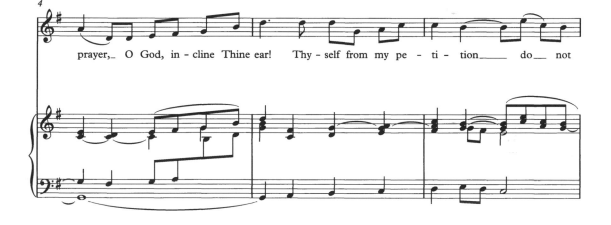

150

93
cry! O God, hear my cry,
cry! O God, hear my cry,
cry! per - plex'd and be -
hear my cry, O God, hear my cry, per -
hear my cry, O God, hear my cry,
98
per - plex'd and be - wil - der'd, O God, hear my
per - plex'd and be - wil - der'd, O God, hear my
- wil - der'd, O God, hear my cry, O
- plex'd and be - wil - der'd, O God,
O God, O God,

Con un poco più di moto

164

far a-way would I rove, a-way would I rove, far a-way!

far a-way, far a-way would I rove, a-way would I rove, far a-way! In the

-way would I rove, far a-way would I rove, far a-way!

-way, far a-way, far a-way would I rove, far a-way!

In the wil-der-ness build me a nest, And re-main there for ev-er at rest,

wil-der-ness build me a nest, And re-main there for ev-er at rest, re-

In the wil-der-ness build me a nest, And re-main there for ev-er at

far a-way! In the

AVE VERUM CORPUS
K.618

WOLFGANG AMADEUS MOZART
edited by Ralph Allwood and David Hill

Dedicated to C.V. Stanford and the members of the Bach Choir

BLEST PAIR OF SIRENS
AN ODE

Text by
John Milton

C. HUBERT H. PARRY

180

188

198

200

I WAS GLAD WHEN THEY SAID UNTO ME

Psalm cxxii, 1-3,6,7

C. HUBERT H. PARRY

Queen's Scholars of Westminster School

Vi - vat Re - gi - na!

Vi - vat Re - gi - na E - li - za - be - tha! vi - vat! vi - vat! vi - vat!

* When the traditional 'Vivats' are impracticable a cut can be made from * to letter **G** on page 212.

† A Fanfare may be interpolated here if required.

SANCTUS

from the *German Mass (Deutsche Messe, D872)*

FRANZ SCHUBERT

GOD SO LOVED THE WORLD

from *The Crucifixion*

John iii, 16,17

JOHN STAINER

only be - got - ten Son, that who - so be - liev - eth, be -

- liev - eth in Him should not per - ish, should not

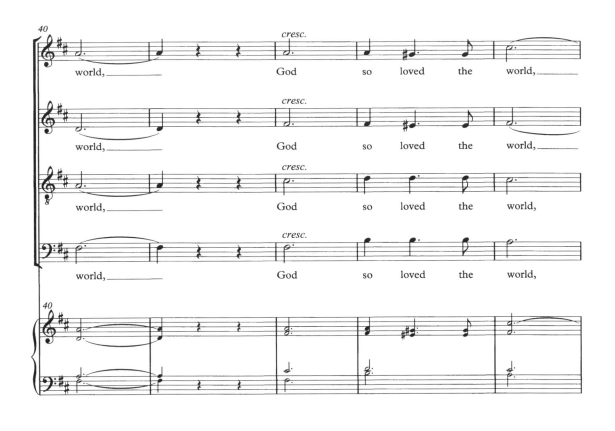

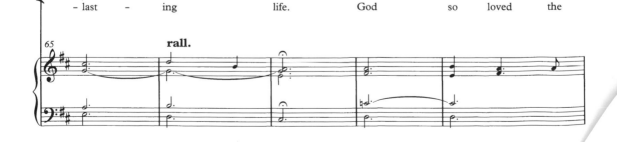

according to conventional theory, are very remote and super-luminous. From all this we can learn more about the evolution of the universe. We can look back to the early period in its history, and as you would expect, we find fewer galaxies and more intergalactic material than is the case now. As we come closer to the present, by studying objects whose light has not taken so long to reach us, we find more galaxies and less intergalactic material.

It is very clear, then, that space is by no means empty. There is a tremendous amount of material spread between the stars and star-systems.

40 Planets — or Brown Dwarfs?

In August 1988 I attended the 20th General Assembly of the International Astronomical Union, which that year was held at Baltimore in the United States. The IAU — the controlling body of world astronomy — meets every three years, and the Assemblies are always fascinating. On this occasion there was a great deal of discussion about 'new planets', and some highly sensational reports found their way into the British and American daily newspapers. Since these reports bore little resemblance to the true facts, it may be as well to try to put the record straight!

To recapitulate: we must always bear in mind that our Sun is a perfectly normal star, one of around 100,000 million in our Galaxy alone, so that there is no reason to assume that it is unique in being attended by a family of planets. We have every reason to believe that other planetary systems exist, but they are difficult to detect because of their immense distances from us. A planet is much smaller than a normal star, and has no light of its own. Trying to observe one in a remote system is rather like an Earth-based astronomer doing his best to detect a glow-worm an inch or two from a powerful searchlight set up on the surface of the Moon.

There have been various cases of faint low-mass stars which show 'wobbles' in their individual movements which could be attributed to the presence of large orbiting planets, but the results can hardly be classed as conclusive. A different approach has been followed by Dr David Latham and his team from the Center for Astrophysics at Cambridge, Massachusetts. They have concentrated upon radial velocities, i.e. towards or away movements. An approaching star will have

ARTIST'S IMPRESSION (BY PAUL DOHERTY) OF A BROWN DWARF SYSTEM

its spectral lines moved over towards the short-wave or blue end of the spectrum; with a receding star, the shift will be to the red. (I wonder how many times in this book I have referred to the Doppler effect? I apologize for the repetition, but it really is a vital part of the present story.) With a single star, the radial velocity will be constant; if there is orbital motion with a close companion body, the lines will oscillate around their mean position.

Latham and his team have been using the latest electronic devices, together with a 61-inch reflecting telescope, to measure stellar radial velocities, and over the past seven or eight years they have made thousands of measurements. Recently they built a new optical fibre-feed system so that they could take the heavy spectrograph off the telescope itself, thereby eliminating many of the usual potential errors. On the first good night of observation with this new system they decided to check on some 'standard' stars, for which many previous measurements had been made. One of these was an undistinguished solar-type star, HD 114762, which is 90 light-years away and is of the seventh magnitude, rather below naked-eye visibility. It is not very unlike the Sun, though apparently rather older. Surprisingly, they found that there was a systematic variation in the radial velocity, fitting an orbital period for an invisible companion of 84.17 days and an amplitude of 533 metres per second. From these results it was possible to work out that the companion was about ten times as massive as Jupiter, the senior member of our own planetary system, and that it was about as far from its parent star as Mercury is from the Sun — that is to say, between 30 and 40 million miles.

But assuming that the object really exists, is it a massive planet or a low-mass star? 'There's an ambiguity about the mass, ' Dr Latham told me, 'because we don't know the angle from which we're viewing the orbit. If it's edge-on, so that all the velocity is represented by orbital motion, then the mass could be as low as 1 per cent that of the Sun, or 10 times that of Jupiter. That would make it roughly on the dividing line between the most massive possible planet and the smallest-mass star — a kind of star known as a Brown Dwarf, a 'failed' star which is not massive enough to trigger off nuclear reactions in its core, and therefore cannot sustain any light output for a long period on the cosmical time-scale. Unfortunately, this dividing line is rather fuzzy, and astronomers cannot agree about what you should call a planet and what you should call a Brown Dwarf.'

Obviously the whole situation is decidedly uncertain, and in any case the orbiting body cannot be in the least like the Earth. Dr Latham himself inclines to the view that we are dealing with a Brown Dwarf, but, as he points out, from the viewpoint of life it hardly matters. 'We're a long way from finding other Earths', he comments. 'Earthlike planets are hundreds of times less massive than the object we've found, and our techniques don't come anywhere near tracking them down.'

Independent confirmation has come from the Coravel group of researchers in Switzerland. Using data obtained at the Haute-Provence Observatory in France, they have derived a period of 83.89 days and an amplitude of 726 metres per second, so that the agreement is remarkably good.

At Baltimore I also spoke with Dr Bruce Campbell, of the University of Victoria in Canada, who has developed a new gas-cell technique to superimpose many narrow spectral lines on to stellar spectra to act as comparisons. The light from the target star is passed through a tube containing the highly toxic gas hydrogen fluoride, which eliminates errors due to flexure of the equipment and other instrumental effects. The standard possible error has been reduced by a factor of nearly 100 from earlier techniques, yielding amplitude resolutions down to 13 metres per second. 'This opens the possibility of detecting companions to solar-type stars at a lower level than previously detectable,' was Dr Campbell's comment.

Of the eighteen stars so far examined in this way, nine have shown velocity trends which suggest companions in the mass range of from 1 to 10 Jupiters, which is too low for the objects to be Brown Dwarfs. In one case, the naked-eye star Alrai or Gamma Cephei, the invisible companion seems to be no more than $1\frac{1}{2}$ times the mass of Jupiter.

What can we infer from all this?

Admittedly the results are still tentative, and are at an early stage, but if they can be confirmed they will show that planetary companions of solar-type stars are common enough. Yet we must be wary of jumping to conclusions, and there was absolutely no justification for one British newspaper headline to the effect that 'a billion planets had been discovered in the Galaxy'!

We must await future developments. All we can really say at the moment is that evidence for extra-solar planetary systems is growing, and this in turn confirms that we have no right to claim that we are alone in the Galaxy.

Index

This book is due for return on or before the last date shown below.